CW01645548

Rachel Garton is a consultant solicitor for Nexa Law, specialising in property dispute resolution.

Her work comprises of all areas of commercial and residential property litigation and landlord and tenant matters, including: tenants right to first refusal, residential leasehold enfranchisement, service charges, lease renewal litigation, commercial and residential possession proceedings and debt recovery.

She has a niche specialism in service charge disputes and has dealt with numerous service charge disputes from commercial and residential clients over the last 15 years as well as delivering a number of seminars on this topic for MBL Seminars.

A Practical Guide to Commercial Property Service Charges

A Practical Guide to Commercial Property Service Charges

Rachel Garton
BSC (Hons), LL.Dip, LL.PgDip

Law Brief Publishing

© Rachel Garton

All rights reserved. No part of this publication may be reproduced, stored in a retrieval system, or transmitted, in any form or by any means, electronic, mechanical, photocopying, recording or otherwise, without the prior permission of the publisher.

Excerpts from judgments and statutes are Crown copyright. Any Crown Copyright material is reproduced with the permission of the Controller of OPSI and the King's Printer for Scotland. Some quotations may be licensed under the terms of the Open Government Licence (http://www.nationalarchives.gov.uk/doc/open-government-licence/version/3).

Cover image © iStockphoto.com/CHUNYIP WONG

The information in this book was believed to be correct at the time of writing. All content is for information purposes only and is not intended as legal advice. No liability is accepted by either the publisher or author for any errors or omissions (whether negligent or not) that it may contain. Professional advice should always be obtained before applying any information to particular circumstances.

Published 2023 by Law Brief Publishing, an imprint of Law Brief Publishing Ltd
30 The Parks
Minehead
Somerset
TA24 8BT

www.lawbriefpublishing.com

Paperback: 978-1-914608-83-4

To Byron, Lilah, Sawyer, Ethan,
Jacob, Ethan and Ember

PREFACE

With the number of commercial service charge disputes rising, this work is intended to serve as a simple guide to the key issues to practitioners. Each chapter provides insight into points that commonly arise and aims to provide guidance necessary to assist in a commercial service charge dispute.

Commercial service charge disputes arise due to a number of issues. The main reason is that there is an inherent conflict of interest between landlords and tenants where service charges are concerned. Landlords want tenants to pay as much as possible towards repairs through service charges so they can receive as much rent as possible without having to make deductions. Tenants want the opposite. They want to pay as little as possible on top of the rent they are already paying. Further both parties are likely to have different views on what is an appropriate standard of repair and to what extent works are necessary.

There is a more limited scope for challenging commercial service charges than residential service charges as they are not subject to the same statutory controls. The tenant's liability to pay service charges as well as the landlord's obligation to do works and charge service charges are entirely contractual.

As there is very limited statutory intervention with commercial service charges, the parties can negotiate the terms of service charge provisions between themselves. This in itself can lead to some issues as often one party will have more bargaining power than the other and will dictate the wording of the service charge provisions in the lease.

Although commercial service charges are not subject to statutory control, there is the RICS 2018 Professional Statement ('the Code') which embodies best practice. Professionals need to consider the Code as if they fail to do so without good reason it leaves them vulnerable to claims of professional negligence.

The main types of commercial service charge disputes that arise are as follows:

1. A dispute between tenants

2. A dispute between the landlord and tenant because the tenant does not consider that they are liable to pay the service charges. This is usually as they believe the landlord has not complied with the requirements under the lease or the works carried out are not covered by the service charge provisions in the lease.

3. A dispute between the landlord and tenant because the tenant does not consider the service charges are reasonable.

4. A dispute between the landlord and tenant as the tenant simply is unable to pay the charges or refuses to do so.

A dispute between the tenants is usually a matter that needs to be referred to the managing agent to be dealt with. For this reason, this book focuses on disputes between landlords and tenants and what a practitioner needs to consider when advising or dealing with these kinds of commercial service charge disputes.

This book endeavours to summarise the current law on commercial service charges as of 30 April 2023. It firstly deals with general principles and then focuses on those areas particularly applicable to commercial service charges. It ends by dealing with service charge disputes, the possible remedies available and possible future changes in the legislation.

Rachel Garton
June 2023

CONTENTS

PART ONE

GENERAL PRINCIPLES APPLICABLE TO SERVICE CHARGES

Part 1 of this book aims to provide guidance on some general principles that practitioners, landlord and tenants should be aware of when dealing with residential service charges. The main area discussed is the importance of wording of the service charge clause and what should be included and provided for within that wording.

Part 1 then progresses to discuss the importance of complying with the requirements under the service charge provisions and other factors which may be considered in assession if service charges are payable.

The principles set out are based on both commercial and residential property case law and the thought to apply to both sectors. Whether each principle applies will depend on the facts of the particular case.

CHAPTER ONE

THE CONSTRUCTION OF THE SERVICE CHARGE CLAUSE

Introduction

The drafting of a service charge clause is paramount. Unlike residential service charges, commercial service charges are not subject to statutory controls and the service charge clause needs to be appropriately drafted. A Court will look at the wording of the lease as a starting point for dealing with most disputes. In addition, a badly drafted service charge clause can lead to numerous disputes regarding interpretation which could be avoided.

The main elements of a service charge clause

The main elements of a service charge clause should be as follows: -

1. A definition of the services to be carried out.

2. Details of the landlord's obligation to provide the services.

3. Details of the tenant's obligation to contribute to the costs of providing those services.

4. The mechanics of the service charge.

Defining the services

This is usually firstly a list of services which the landlord must provide for the communal areas of the property and secondly a list of services which the landlord can but is not obliged to provide.

The services specified will depend on what is applicable to the particular property, but it should be as detailed a list as possible and aim to cover all the services that could be provided.

The lease may also contain a sweeper clause. The purpose of a sweeper clause is to effectively cover any additional services the landlord may provide which are not specified in the list of services contained in the main service charge clause.

Practitioners should be wary of the inclusion and drafting of sweeper clauses and aim to restrict the clause to being tied to the categories of services that they have specified in the main clause. Sweeper clauses are construed quite restrictively, and there is no guarantee that the inclusion of a sweeper clause will allow the landlord to recover costs for any services that become necessary, or they decide to carry out that are outside of the those provided for.

Relevant Cases

Fluor Daniel Properties Limited v Shortlands Investments Limited [2001]

Provided that sweeper clauses shouldn't be used to try and recover service charges for a service which the landlord has simply failed to provide for in the service charge clause in error.

Boldmark Limited v Cohan and another [1986]

It was held that the landlords attempt to claim interest that was incurred as a result of borrowing to finance the provision of services was not recoverable under a sweeper clause that provided for recovery of service charges for general administration and management of the property.

Excluded Services

Certain services are likely to be excluded from the calculation of a service charge.

a. Original Setting-up costs for the development

   If the landlord has incurred costs in setting up the development the tenants should not be liable to pay the costs of these set up costs. This has been held to include providing initial items such as cleaning equipment for use in common parts of the development.

b. The costs of repairing latent and/or inherent defects

   The tenant will not want to bear the cost of repairing any defects in the construction of the development. A tenant may agree to accept that these costs fall within the service s due if there is an obligation on the landlord to enforce its rights against the original party responsible for the defect i.e., the contractor or engineer. However, the question would then be whether the tenant is responsible for the costs of this enforcement action against the third party.

c. The landlord's costs in relation to breaches of covenants by tenants.

Tenants will wish to exclude any costs incurred by the landlord in pursuing a different tenant or tenants for failure to pay the service charge due or breaches of covenant. This would seem unjust if the tenant liable to pay the costs is up to date on their payments and has not breached the lease.

Relevant Cases

St Modwen Developments (Edmonton) Limited v Tesco Stores Limited (2006)

The costs in relation to the breaches of covenants by tenants will not be excluded automatically.

Plantation Wharf Management Company Limited v Jackson & Another (2011)

The Upper Tribunal had to decide whether a lease must contain an express reference to 'legal costs' for the landlord to recover its legal costs of taking action against defaulting tenants through service charges. It was held the legal costs could be recovered even though the service charge clause did not set out that legal costs were payable. Despite the failure of the lease to reference legal costs, it was decided that the legal costs could be recovered on a fair construction of the lease.

d. Costs of rent collection

Tenants may want to try and exclude this expense from the service charge provisions. However, if the managing agents have the right to charge a single management fee under the lease that is inclusive of rent collection it is going to be more difficult for the tenant to argue it should be excluded.

e. Costs relating to empty lettable units.

In developments there can sometimes be one of more units that are empty. Tenants need to ensure that the landlord is liable to contribute the part of the service charge that would have been payable by the tenant of the unlet unit. Whether this is possible is likely to depend on the method of apportioning the rent that has been adopted for the development. Apportionment of service charges is discussed later in this book.

<u>Services that should be credited to the service charges paid.</u>

1. <u>Any generated income</u>

If there is anything in the development that is generating an income a tenant will want the income generated to be credited to the service charges due. An example of generated income would be a car park in a centre that charges money for the public to use. In these circumstances, the Code gives the option of the landlord including both the income and cost of upkeep of the car park in the service charge provisions or for the landlord to exclude both the costs and the income from the tenant's service charge provisions.

Another example would be where there are utilities that belong to a third party which are shared between the centre or development and the adjoining property. If the third party which is using the utilities is under an obligation to the landlord to contribute to the cost of repairing those utilities, any sums paid by that third party should be credited to the service charges due from the tenants.

2. **Insurance money**

There is some overlap between service charges and insurance money. When insurance money is received in respect of items that the tenants are responsible for under the service charge provisions, the insurance money should be credited to the service charge account.

One of the common issues is that when there has been damage by an uninsured risk, the landlord will usually have to continue with their obligation under the lease such as providing the services and carrying out repairs. Similarly, the tenant will still be liable to pay for those services carried out. This can cause issues when the property has been substantially damaged and, in some circumstances, no longer useable. The service charge provisions therefore need to be carefully drafted to cover such scenarios.

Landlord's obligation to provide the services

It is crucial that a service charge clause sets out that the landlord is obliged to carry out the services detailed. If not, a tenant is potentially left living in a property where the common areas may fall into disrepair.

There is sometimes an obligation on a landlord to carry out some services and then a clause that sets out the services the landlord can provide if they choose. In respect of the latter the tenant will be under an obligation to pay for those services if carried out, but the landlord does not have to carry out those services.

The clause can set out that the landlord's obligation to carry out the works are conditional on the tenant paying the service charge due.

However, practitioners should be aware that this may not be enforceable if other tenant have paid their service charge contributions. In addition, a Court is likely to be reluctant to allow a landlord to withhold services which are considered essential.

Relevant Case Law

Yorkbrook Investments Limited -v- Batten [1986]

The landlord's covenant to provide services began: "Subject to the Lessee paying the Maintenance Contributions pursuant to the obligations under Clause 4 hereof". The tenant withheld their payment of the service charges in respect of the maintenance contributions as they believed the landlord was in breach of its obligations under the lease. It was held that despite the tenant's non-payment the landlord was still under an obligation to provide the services and that the wording of the clause did not amount to a condition precedent when the lease was read as a whole.

Tenant's obligation to contribute to the service charge

The service charge provisions should state that the tenant is obliged to pay for the services specified and also deal with the below.

The apportionment of the service charge

The apportionment of service charges between the tenant is usually one of the following:

- By way of fixed proportions. This method provides certainty. However, it is quite inflexible and can be unfair if the building is later developed/extended. If the fixed proportion is a percentage, tenants should also be wary as if any of the flats in the property are not let, they are likely to have to pay a higher sum towards the service charges unless provision has been specifically made for this occurrence.

- The tenant is asked to pay a fair proportion. This method of apportionment is likely to lead to disputes because what is 'fair' is open for interpretation. What a landlord and tenant consider to be a fair proportion is likely to differ.

- By reference to floor areas. Although to a degree this method seems fairer it can sometimes be difficult to calculate.

- By reference to rateable value. Again, this seems one of the fairer methods but can cause problems if the property is a new build and no rateable values have been set or in cases where there have been any improvements to the property.

As can be seen from the above, specifying how service charges are to be apportioned is a difficult task. Disputes can arise no matter which method is used, and all practitioners can do is try and choose the method which appears to be the most fair and reasonable for the particular property.

Relevant case

Aviva Investors Ground Rent GP Ltd and another v Williams and others [2021]

A tenant's lease required them to pay service charges that was stated to be a fixed percentage of a proportion to be reasonably determined by the landlord. The Court of Appeal held that section 27A (6) of the Act rendered the landlord's discretion void. The discretion was transferred to the First Tier Tribunal to determine the proportion of the service charge.

How tenants are to pay the service charges

The service charge clause needs to set out how the tenant is to pay the service charges. The usual way is for the tenant to make quarterly payments on account during each service charge year.

The clause should also provide for any additional sums that may become due at the year-end due to a shortfall once the service charge accounts have been finalised or any surplus of funds at the year end.

The Mechanics of the Service Charge

For any workable service charge clause there needs to be provision for the following: -

1. The Service charge year – the tenant needs to know the period for the service charge accounts are to be prepared.

2. Provision for the statement of account to be prepared. This needs to set out who is to prepare the statement and who is to certify the statement. It is important that the landlord then follows this requirement to avoid the statement of account being invalid and providing a defence to the payment of the service charges that have arisen.

3. A timetable for preparing the service charge accounts. This can just be a requirement for the landlord to provide the accounts as soon as reasonably possible if the landlord is concerned about being tied down to a strict period. The important thing for landlords to note is that there shouldn't be excessive delay

and a period of approx. 4 months after the end of the service charge year is usually deemed reasonable.

4. How any disputes regarding the service charges are to be dealt with. This will normally set out if there is to be a referral to a third party.

Summary

Practitioners need to take great care when drafting the service charges provisions in a lease. They should take into account the 4 areas set out above and also ensure that they include as many services as possible as well as account for all possible scenarios. It is a difficult task but the more detail that is provided and the clearer the provisions are at the outset will lead to less disputes over interpretation.

CHAPTER TWO

SINKING OR RESERVE FUNDS

Introduction

There may be provisions in a lease that relate to a sinking fund or a reserve fund. The purpose of these funds is to provide for substantial items of expenditure in relation to the service charge. These clauses should be carefully drafted, and the two types of funds not confused. It is important to note that if there is no provision in the lease for a sinking or reserve fund, the landlord is not able to use funds in this way.

Sinking Funds

These funds are intended to cover the repair or replacement of major items of disrepair such as to equipment. It could be described as a replacement fund which is there ready to cover the repair or replacement of major items when needed. The use of a sinking fund can avoid the tenants getting a large bill for major works that they may not be able to afford. For this reason, it can avoid the risk of tenants becoming insolvent.

Reserve Funds

These funds are intended to cover more regular items of expenditure. They are still likely to be major items of expenditure but may be items such as external decoration. It is an expense that is not unexpected, and the parties have simply built up a fund to pay for this anticipated expenditure so they are not hit with a hefty bill. It helps to even out fluctuations in the annual service charges due from the tenant from year to year and makes it easier for the parties to manage expenditure. This again makes it less likely that the tenants can't afford the expenditure.

Issues that arise with the use of Sinking and Reserve Funds

In practice, leases leave the definition and purposes of the funds as very unclear so much so that it is often not clear if a sinking or a reserve fund is to be created. This can leave it more open to tenants to dispute the landlord can use the fund for the works carried out and/or for the tenants to argue that there has been a misappropriation of funds.

A further issue in Commercial Property is that the sums held in the sinking or reserve fund will normally be expressed to be held on trust, in their respective shares, by the landlord for the tenants of the development, in their respective shares. As the funds are held on trust it can lead to tax consequences for the tenants.

The tax consequences and the burdens of administering the fund, have meant that sinking and reserve funds have become less popular in recent years. However, they are still used where it is still considered appropriate to spread the costs for major items of expenditure or anticipated major costs. They will also still appear in older leases so practitioners need to be aware of the funds and when they can be used.

Large commercial tenants are less likely to request a sinking or reserve fund than smaller tenants as they are more likely to be able to cope with a large expenditure than a smaller tenant who may not have the funds to cover a replacement of a major item in the premises.

Relevant Case Law

Brown's Operating System Services V Southwark Roman Catholic Diocesan Corporation [2007]

The lease did not contain an express provision for a reserve or sinking fund. The tenant covenanted to pay a service charge being a contribution towards the 'total service cost' to include 'such sum as the landlord shall ... think fit as being a reasonable provision for expenditure likely to be incurred in the future in connection with the matters mentioned in this Schedule'.

The landlord would build up a surplus of the service charge monies received to put towards future expenditure as and when it was necessary. The tenant thought he was building up a credit on his account so that at some point he would not have to pay any charges and effectively would have a service charge holiday.

When the tenant understood the landlord's position, he exercised an option to terminate his lease and withheld the last 2 quarters rent due. The landlord took action for recovery of the sims due arguing he had a right to retain the service charge money received for future expenditure.

It was held that in the absence of express provisions for a reserve or sinking fund, any surplus monies received by the landlord on account of future expenditure, must be returned to that tenant at the end of the term of the lease, or in this case on the expiry of the break notice served.

The RICS 2018 Professional Statement does not require that a sinking fund or a reserve fund be used in a lease. It does, however, provide that monies paid by the tenants into any sinking or reserve fund must be held by the landlord in one or more separate discrete (or virtual) accounts, in trust for the occupiers, and separate from the landlord's own monies, with interest on the account accruing to the service charge account.

Summary

If parties want to use a reserve or sinking fund, they need to make provision for a fund in the lease. As the purpose of each type of fund is very different, practitioners need to ensure that there is clear drafting setting out which fund is to be used and as far as possible what items the sums obtained are looking to fund.

CHAPTER THREE

THE COURT'S INTERPRETATION OF A SERVICE CHARGE CLAUSE

Introduction

If a Court is to consider a service charge dispute, they will examine the service charge provisions in the lease to come to a conclusion. This chapter aims to provide case law for how the Court have interpreted service charge provisions previously.

The Court's Interpretation

A Court is unlikely to imply a term into a service charge clause or construe the express terms of a service charge clause in a different way to take into consideration commercial sense or to remedy the fact that a party has signed up to a bad deal.

Relevant cases

Arnold v Britton [2005]

The lease contained a service charge clause which provided for a fixed annual charge of £90 for the first year of the term and it was to increase each subsequent year by 10% on a £1 basis. This meant that in 2072, the tenants would be liable to pay a service charge for over £550,000.

The tenants argued this could not have been what was intended. The court held that the service charge clause was clear, and it was not for the Court to step in and imply a term to prevent the tenant from having to pay the contractual terms due. The fact it was a really bad deal for the tenants was irrelevant in interpreting the clause.

Marks & Spencers Plc v BMP Paribas Securities Trust Company (Jersey) Limited [2015]

The lease contained a break clause which had a pre-condition that there should be no rent arrears. The tenant exercised their right under the break to terminate the lease on 24 January 2012. The rent was due on the usual quarter dates and the tenant paid the full quarters rent on 25 December 2011 in order to comply with the pre-condition that there should be no rent arrears. The tenant then requested the overpayment of rent for the period after the lease was terminated from 25 January 2012 to 24 March 2012. It was held that the landlord did not have to refund the overpayment for when the tenant was no longer in occupation as there was no express obligation for the landlord to do so.

Summary

The drafting of the service charge clauses is crucial to ensure that the provision of services and payment for those services runs smoothly. Neither party is likely to be able to imply a term into the service charge clause at a later date because they were unsure of the meaning and/or have realised they have signed up to a bad deal. Nor is a landlord likely to be able to claim service charges for services which they have omitted from the drafting in error.

CHAPTER FOUR

COMPLYING WITH THE MECHANICS OF A SERVICE CHARGE CLAUSE

Introduction

Having set out the mechanics of the service charge in the lease, the parties and in particular the landlord needs to ensure they comply with any requirements in the lease to ensure they can recover service charges from the tenant and avoid a dispute over liability.

Contractual machinery

If a lease provides contractual machinery, the landlord must comply with this machinery, or the service charges are unlikely to be payable. Contractual machinery is likely to be in relation to the provision of service charge accounts and/or service charge estimates, how service charges payments are to be held and dates payment are to be made.

A number of cases have shown that a landlord will need to rectify any error they have made by failing to comply with the requirements of a service charge clause and also that the landlord may not be able to recover service charges from tenants if the contractual machinery has not been observed.

A common issue is when a managing agent takes over the running of a property and fails to review the lease and the requirements thereunder prior to using the accounting equipment/programmes they currently own. It may seem more time intensive to a landlord or a management company in the short term to review the leases of the development and implement any requirements but in the long term it can prevent disputes about whether service charges are payable. In turn this can avoid significant losses for the landlord/management company if the service charges are not deemed recoverable.

Relevant cases

St Mary's Mansions Limited v Limegate Investment Co. Limited [2003]

The leases for a block of flats provided for a reserve fund for any anticipated expenditure. The landlord was transferring surplus payments that were being paid into the service charge account into the reserve fund. It was held that as the lease only provided for sums in the reserve fund to be anticipated expenditure only the sums held in the reserve fund for recurring expenditure had been properly allocated. The landlord had to repay or credit any surplus to the tenants at the end of each service charge year. The judge stated that compliance with contractual machinery in the leases is not optional, it is compulsory.

Jacey Property Company Limited v De Sousa [2003]

The landlord sought possession of the property and one of the grounds they were relying on to forfeit the lease was that the tenant had failed to pay the costs due in respect of work carried out to the drains. The lease provided that the tenant was to pay a proper and fair portion as determined by the landlord's surveyor of the expense of repairing, renewing and rebuilding the sewers and drains. The landlord had claimed service charges from the tenant for the works carried out, but the landlord had the portion payable determined by their solicitor not their surveyor as provided for in the lease. The tenant disputed that the sum was payable as it the potion payable had not been determined by the landlord's surveyor. The tenant was successful, and it was held that it is not for the landlord to decide to use anyone other than a surveyor even if they chose an appropriately skilled person as an alternative. The tenant did not need to contribute to the works carried out on the drains and the landlord could not rely on this ground to terminate the lease.

Barrington v Sloane Properties [2007]

The landlord carried out substantial building works between 2000 and 2003. The leases of the block of flats provided that the tenants would pay 24.24% of the actual costs of the landlord but that the sums due had to be certified annually by the landlord's accountant. The landlord's accountant apportioned and certified the costs of the works for each service charge year on the basis of an estimate of the value of the works carried out. The Court held that the certificates were not binding as the accountant had not taken into consideration the actual costs that the landlord has to pay in each service charge year. The lease had been misinterpreted and the landlord was therefore not entitled to recover the sums due.

Sara & Hossein Asset Holdings Limited v Blacks Outdoor Retail Limited [2020]

A service charge clause in two commercial leases that stated that the landlord should provide to the tenant a certificate "as to the total cost and the sum payable to the tenant" and that that was to be "conclusive" in the absence of "manifest or mathematical error or fraud" was conclusive as to what the tenant was required to pay following certification, but it did not preclude the tenant from later disputing liability.

Summary

Blacks were the tenant of retail premises owned by SHAH and had generally paid around £55,000 in service charges under the lease.

The service charge terms in the lease provided that, at the end of each calendar year, the landlord was obliged to calculate the "total reasonable and proper cost" of the services incurred during that year and to provide the tenant with a certificate of such sums payable.

The service charge liability for 2017/2018 and 2018/2019, certified by SHAH as per the lease, was over £400,000. Blacks challenged the sum through the lower Court.

The Court of Appeal found that in line with the service charge provisions in the leases the landlord's certificate was "conclusive" on both the proportion of the overall service charge payable and whether each service fell within the scope of the service charge clause.

Condition Precedent

A Condition Precedent effectively sets out the events that must occur before liability for service charges can arise. This is similar to contractual machinery but can appear in lease in addition to contractual machinery and again is something that landlords need to be very careful they comply with to avoid a challenge from tenants regarding payment.

Relevant Case

Quirkco Investments Limited -v- Aspray Transport Ltd [2011]

The tenant served a break notice to terminate the lease. The landlord argued the break was ineffective as they had not paid the services charges due in respect of the insurance premium. The lease set out that the landlord should only demand service charges in respect of insurance charges once the landlord had paid the premium. The landlord had not paid the premium when he demanded payment of the charges. The court held that as the landlord had not paid the premium the charges were not due from the tenant. The tenant had validly exercised the break in the lease and the lease would terminate on the date specified in the notice.

Summary

If there are provisions in the lease, they must be strictly complied with. Failure to do is likely to result in either a further administrative burden in trying to rectify the error or a financial loss.

CHAPTER FIVE

FACTORS APPLICABLE TO BOTH COMMERCIAL AND RESIDENTIAL PROPERTY IN CONSIDERING IF SERVICE CHARGES ARE PAYABLE

Introduction

It is common sense that the landlord can only claim costs by way of service charges for the services specified in the lease. A landlord should therefore ensure that he only carries out works for which he can recover payment and a tenant should check that the landlord isn't charging them for works outside of the that payable under the service charge clause. As set out in Chapter 1, the landlord may try and rely on sweeper clauses but there is no guarantee this will be successful.

In addition to whether the works are covered under the service charge clause, landlords also need to ensure that they take into consideration/ be aware of the following.

Repairs or Improvements

Sometimes improvements can be covered in the service charge clause. Whether they are included usually comes down to the bargaining power of the parties. Usually, they will be excluded, and landlords need to be careful that service charges claimed are for repairs not improvements, if improvements are not covered under the service charge clause. There are frequent disputes about what is a repair and what is an improvement, and this area of law is far from clear. A few cases are set out below to aid in assessing whether works are an improvement or a repair, but it is stressed that any finding by a Court will be highly dependent on the facts of the particular case.

Relevant Cases

Fluor Daniel Properties Limited v Shortlands Investments Limited [2001]

The landlord replaced the air conditioning units. The Court held this was an improvement not a repair. However, it is important to note that the air conditioning unit was still working when it was replaced. The Court may have held the replacement of the air conditioning unit to be a repair if the air conditioning unit had been in a state of disrepair and needed replacing.

Craighead v Home for Islington Ltd [2010]

It was held that replacement single glaze windows with double glazed windows were repairs not improvements. On first thought, you would consider this an improvement as it is effectively an upgrade. However, now all new homes have double glazed windows as standard, and it is reasonable if a landlord is going to repair single glaze windows to upgrade them to what is now the norm.

Tedworth North Management Limited v Miller [2016]

The Court held that wooden frames being replaced with metal frames was an improvement. They said that the old frames only needed small scale repair not replacing. The works went above what was needed in the circumstances.

Service Charge Cap

Service charges can be capped imposing a restriction on the amount that can be charged by a landlord to the tenant in any service charge year. If there is a service charge cap in place, landlords should not try and get round this restriction.

A cap may be subject to increase in accordance with the *Retail Prices Index (RPI)* or a similar mechanism.

Tenants should be aware that, depending on the drafting of the cap provision, the service charge may actually be fixed at the capped amount, so that what the tenant anticipates being the maximum that can be charged, is, in fact, the actual figure charged.

Landlords should be aware that agreeing to a service charge cap for a tenant can lead to irrecoverable service costs. If a particular tenant's service charge payments are capped, the landlord (or management company) is unlikely to be able to require the other tenants to pay any amounts that cannot be charged to the tenant with the benefit of the cap. This will leave a shortfall between the service costs and the amount that can be collected from the tenants.

Relevant Case

Princes House Ltd & Another v Distinctive Clubs Ltd [2007].

The service charge clause included a cap on the recovery in the first 5 years of the lease, The landlord informed the tenant that they would be carrying out works to the roof within the first 5 years. The landlord then stated the works would take longer than envisaged and would not be within the first 5 years. The landlord then looked to claim the costs in full as they had avoided the service charge cap. The tenant disputed the sums were due as they were a result of the landlord purposely delaying. The landlord's defence was that their obligation to do the works was qualified by a liability clause stating that the landlord would not be liable to the tenant in respect of their failure to carry out maintenance and repair duties until the tenant had notified the landlord of such a failure. The landlord argued that the tenant had not sent any notification to them. It was held that the landlord was fully aware of the need to do the works as they had informed the tenant of their intention to carry out the works. The landlord could not now rely on the liability clause. The works should have been carried out within the 5-year window and were subject to the service charge cap. The landlord could not simply delay works to avoid the cap.

Estoppel by convention

The general rule of interpretation of a service charge clause is set out in the chapters above i.e., if the landlord does not comply with the service charge provisions strictly, the service charges are unlikely to be due. However, there is the possibility of an argument in some rare cases that if a tenant has conceded the landlord's failure to comply with the service charges provisions for a duration of time the tenant is estopped from objecting to this error.

Relevant Case

Admiralty Park Management Limited v Ojo [2016]

There was an error in the landlord's calculations of service charge due and they sent non-compliant service charge demands to the tenants for a period of 5 years from 2009 to 2014. The lease provided that the service charge payable should be calculated by dividing the total charge for each block of flats by the number of flats within that block. Instead, the landlord had been dividing the total charge for the whole estate by the number of flats in the estate. The number of flats in each block varied so the landlord had been using the wrong apportionment. Although the tenant had been paying the sums demanded since 2009, he stopped paying in 2014 and argued the sums claimed were not payable due to the landlord's error. It was held that the sums claimed were still payable. The tenant was estopped by convention from objecting as they had accepted the error without protest for several years. This case was a fascinating development as it showed it is possible for a party's conduct to effectively vary the requirements under the lease. Despite this case, an argument on estoppel by convention should be raised with caution. It will be highly dependent on the facts and in particular how long the error has been ongoing and when the tenant became aware of the error.

Summary

When looking to carry out works under the lease, the landlord needs to double check that the costs that they are looking to recover are covered by the provisions in the lease and are also that they are likely to be able to recover the sums claimed in light of the principles above. The general principles discussed need to be looked at alongside the facts of the case.

PART TWO

PRINCIPLES APPLICABLE TO COMMERCIAL SERVICE CHARGES

Part 1 has dealt with the general law and some general principles on service charge clauses. These issues apply to commercial and residential service charges equally and are a crucial starting point. Part 2 aims to deal with some key considerations when dealing with commercial service charges and the application of the Code. The matters dealt with are not an exhaustive list of what a practitioner should consider but aim to aid and assist in considering commercial service charges disputes.

CHAPTER SIX

FACTORS TO CONSIDER IN DETERMINING WHETHER COMMERCIAL SERVICE CHARGES CLAIMED ARE PAYABLE UNDER THE LEASE

Introduction

When a tenant approaches a professional/practitioner regarding a commercial service charge dispute, there may be some additional points to consider depending on the nature of the dispute. This chapter considers how to deal with disputes relating to whether charges are reasonable. It should be read in conjunction with the considerations set out in Part 1 of this book.

Do the service charge costs have to be reasonable?

There is no legislation stating that service charges rendered by the landlord have to be reasonable.

When negotiating the terms of the service charge provisions, a tenant is likely to ask for the service charges provisions to be quantified by the requirement for the landlord to act reasonably and for the charges to be reasonable. A tenant may also ask for other requirements to be imposed on the landlord such as for the landlord to proceed economically and efficiently or that the landlord must obtain a number of estimates for any works to be carried out.

If the requirement of 'reasonableness' is set out in the lease, then the landlord must be reasonable, or the tenant can apply to the Court disputing the service charges on the grounds of reasonableness. To determine if the service charges claimed are reasonable, the Court is likely to look at other cost estimates for the work carried out. The Court will not necessarily find that the landlord has acted unreasonably if they have not employed the contractor that provided the lowest estimate. The Court will consider what is reasonable in all the circumstances and if the landlord has acted reasonably in adopting the appropriate procedures in deciding who to instruct to carry out the works.

If there is a requirement for a landlord to act economically or efficiently, the landlord needs to manage the property economically and efficiently and ensure value for money for the tenants by spending as little as reasonably practical on the works required.

The question is whether 'reasonableness' can be implied when it is not expressly set out in the lease. At the current time this issue is not clear-cut but it appears that the Court is likely to imply that even in the absence of an express provision, the costs claimed should be reasonable. The justification for this implication is that a landlord should not have an unfettered discretion and be able to employ the most expensive contractor with no good reason and then charge this to the tenants. However, if a service charge clause includes another term in respect of the service charge provisions such as 'properly' or 'efficiently' then reasonableness may not be implied as the parties have considered and expressly stated the requirements that a landlord must follow in imposing service charges.

Relevant Cases

Finchborne v Rodrigues [1976]

There was not express requirement for the tenant to be reasonable. The Court of Appeal stated that it could be implied that the costs claimed were fair and reasonable as it could not be intended that the landlord should have an 'unfettered discretion' to adopt the highest conceivable standard and to charge the tenant with it.

Havenbridge v Boston Dyers [1994]

The tenant was obliged to refund insurance premiums that had been 'properly' incurred by the landlord. The Court held that the requirement of 'properly' meant simply that the insurer was a reputable company, that the premiums reflected the insurers normal rates, and they were paid in the ordinary course of business. The Court did not imply the term 'reasonable' into the obligation of the landlord despite the case of *Finchborne V Rodrigues [1976]* set out above.

Criterion Buildings Ltd v McKinsey and Company Inc (UK) and another [2021] EWHC 216 (Ch)

This case concerned various leases of office premises near Piccadilly Circus in London. The service charge provisions in the lease enabled the landlord to recover from the tenant and the other occupiers, a contribution towards the costs of providing various services.

The service charge provisions stated that the tenant was to pay a 'due proportion' of the services and expenses set out in the lease. "Due proportion" was defined as:

"A fair proportion to be determined from time to time by the Landlord taking into account the benefit that was derived".

The landlord had calculated the "due proportion" based on respective floor areas occupied by the different tenants.

The tenant withheld part of the service charges payment due which amounted to £2.2 million as they stated that they had been overcharged by the landlord. The tenant argued that:

(1) What the landlord had charged as the "due proportion" did not comply with the lease because it was not "fair" as it did not represent their share of the floor area.

(2) The landlord had not properly operated the provisions regarding sinking and reserve funds or given any justification in demanding contributions to a sinking fund to replace the lifts.

(3) They had carried out works and the value of those works should be offset against sums claimed by the landlord.

The landlord brought a claim against the tenant for the sums due. It was held that it was the tenant who had the burden of establishing that the apportionment adopted by the landlord was unfair; or that the apportionment did not amount to a due proportion as defined by the lease.

The tenant had failed to prove either of the above and the landlord was entitled to decide what was a fair proportion of the service charges.

Length of lease

Courts are reluctant to impose high costs on a tenant with only a short-term interest in the lease and a landlord will need to show works were really necessary before the expiry of the lease.

Relevant cases

Fluor Daniel Properties Limited v Shortlands Investments Limited [2001]

This case has been discussed previously in respect of whether works are and improvement or a repair. Another relevant finding the case was that if a landlord is to act reasonably, they need to have regard to the length of the lease.

Scottish Mutual Assurance Plc v Jardine Public Relations [1999].

The tenant had a 3-year lease with only a few months left to run when the landlord proposed to replace the roof. It was held that the tenant was only required to contribute to the cost of patch repairs to the roof. The replacement of the roof was not necessary before the end of the tenant's lease and it was seen that by doing the works now, the landlord was simply attempting to recover more money from the tenant.

Summary

In considering whether the service charges are reasonable, the specific terms of the lease need to be considered alongside the possibility of an implied right of 'reasonableness'. Regard should also be given to the length of the lease alongside the urgency of the works.

CHAPTER SEVEN

THE IMPACT OF THE SERVICE CHARGE CODE: PROFESSIONAL STATEMENT

Introduction

On 17th September 2018 the RICS published its latest professional statement entitled "*Service Charge in Commercial Properties*" ('the Code'). The statement applies to all service charges across the UK and is applicable to all service charge periods commencing from 1 April 2019. It updates and replaces the 2014 service code practice and formalises the code within the RICS best practice framework. The statement sets out the best practice in the management and the administration of service charge in commercial properties and provides mandatory obligations and there is a general principle of transparency throughout.

There are legal and/or disciplinary consequences for departing from the Code and firms engaged with commercial service charges need to adhere to the Code or they could potentially face disciplinary proceedings. If a professional departs from the recommendations in the Code that use the words "*must*" or "*will*" they will need a justifiable good reason.

Main Aims and Objectives

The four main aims and objectives of the Code are as follows: -

1. To improve general standards and promote best practice, uniformity, fairness and transparency in the management and administration of service charge in commercial property.

2. To ensure timely issue of budgets and year end certificates.

3. To reduce the cause of dispute and provide guidance on dispute resolution.

4. To provide guidance on negotiation, drafting and interpretation of leases in accordance with best practice.

Mandatory Requirements

The Code sets out 9 mandatory requirements. These are considered the minimum acceptable standards of performance and professionals involved with the management of service charge accounts must comply with these mandatory requirements.

The mandatory requirements are as follows: -

1. All expenditure that the owner or manager seeks to recover from the tenants must be in accordance with the terms of the lease.

2. Owners and managers of properties must seek to recover no more than 100% of the proper and actual cost of provisional supply of the services.

3. Owners and managers must ensure that service charge budgets are issued annually to all tenants. The service charge budgets must include an appropriate explanatory commentary.

4. Owners and managers must ensure that a signed statement showing a true and accurate record of the actual expenditure constituting a service charge is provided annually to all tenants.

5. Owners and managers must ensure that a service charge apportionment matrix for their property is provided annually to all tenants.

6. Service charge monies must be held in one or more discreet or virtual bank accounts. This includes a reserve or sinking fund.

7. All interest earned on service charge accounts must be paid to the service charge accounts. This is after appropriate deductions have been made.

8. Where acting on behalf of a tenant, RICS members must advise clients that if a service charge disputes the tenant should only withhold the actual sums that is in dispute.

9. When acting on behalf of a landlord, RICS members must advise their clients that following resolution of a dispute, any service charge that has been raised incorrectly should be adjusted to reflect the error without undue delay.

The Core Principles

If a landlord complies with the mandatory requirements, it is seen that the landlord is acting to an acceptable standard. There are also 24 core principles that underpin and support the mandatory requirements and it is best practice for the landlord to also have regard to all the core principles in the Code.

The RICS appreciates that some of the core principles may be difficult to quantify and has included a caveat that in rare circumstances strict compliance may not always be possible. In these cases, the parties involved will need to judge the appropriate level of compliance with the core principles of the Code.

The more significant core principles are as follows:

1. Services are procured on an appropriate value for money basis. All competitive quotations are obtained, or the costs benchmarked.

2. Owners/managers have the right to set the standards by which their investment will be managed and the duty to manage. However, managers/owners should always consult with occupiers regarding the standard quality of service charge provisions required.

3. Managers/owners should be transparent in demonstrating how they have complied with the principles of the Code.

4. All new leases should include a provision for either party to require the resolution of disputes though alternative dispute resolution. This includes renewal leases.

Interaction of the Code with the lease terms

The starting point for the interpreting the service charge provisions is always the lease, and the landlord must always abide by the lease requirements. The Code is in addition to what is set out in the lease, and it does not override the terms of the lease. The outcome of disputes will come down to the interpretation and clear wording of the lease and the service charge provisions. However, the service charge provisions in the lease should be read in conjunction with the Code to help identify the best interpretation of the lease provisions and ensure compliance with the Code as far as possible.

Some of the core principles of the Code have a direct impact on the lease provisions as they go as far as to exclude specific activities from being eligible for service charge costs. Some of these excluded activities have been discussed earlier in this book in the discussion on defining services. The excluded activities include: -

(a) Any initial costs (including costs of leasing equipment).

(b) Any setting up costs including costs of fitting out and equipping the on-site management offices that are reasonably considered to be part of the original development cost of the property.

(c) Future development costs.

(d) Any improvement costs above the costs of normal maintenance, repair or replacement.

Guidance

The Code also contains guidance on best practice in support of the mandatory requirements and the core principles. Parties should be aware of this guidance and adhere to it where possible. However, parties should take into consideration what is reasonable in each specific circumstance and adherence to the recommendations contained in the guidance is left to professional judgement of the parties involved.

Appendix of the Code

In the appendix of the Code there is a compliance checklist. This is a good guide for any practitioner/professional in this area to use to ensure compliance with the Code.

Relationship of the Code with the Lease Code of 2020

The Lease Code 2020 came into effect on 1 September 2020 and contains a mixture of mandatory requirements as well as best practice for agents or landlords that are RICS members or part of RICS regulated firms.

At Paragraph 5 of Part 3, the Lease Code 2020 states what is considered best practice for lease negotiations. It states that:

1. Landlords should indicate the range of main services.

2. Landlords should provide proper estimates of service charges and insurance payments.

3. Landlords should disclose all other outgoings that the tenant will incur under the lease. An example would be business rates.

4. Landlords should disclose known irregular events that would have a significant impact on the amount of future service charges.

5. Both landlords and tenants should have regard to the Code

6. In so far as practicable in the circumstances, service charge provisions in leases should be drafted considering the mandatory provisions and core principles of the Code.

7. Tenants should ask landlords whether the service charges are being administered in compliance with the Code.

Guidance on Sinking/Reserve Funds

The Code does not require that the lease provides for a sinking or reserve fund. However, the Code does provide that if any monies are paid by the tenants into a sinking or reserve fund the monies must be held by the landlord in one or more separate discrete (or virtual) accounts, in trust for the tenants. The account should be separate from the landlord's own money/accounts and any interest that accrues on that account should be credited to the service charge account.

Conclusion

There is no legislation or statutory requirements in respect of commercial service charges. However, the Code provides some regulatory requirements and guidance. The Code should be carefully considered by professionals/practitioners who draft leases or are involved in advising on service charge provisions in the lease or service charge disputes.

PART THREE

MISCELLANEOUS POINTS TO CONSIDER

There are a number of factors or issues that practitioners should be aware of when dealing with commercial service charges either when drafting the lease or dealing with disputes. These don't directly relate to the construction or interpretation of the service charge clauses but may be relevant when advising a landlord or tenant. Part 3 looks to set out these miscellaneous points that might arise from time to time when dealing with Commercial Service Charges.

CHAPTER EIGHT

TAX AND INDEXATION

Introduction

When looking at obligations in the lease, the parties may want to consider the tax position in respect of payment of service charges and also whether the service charges are indexed and the likely impact of any indexation.

Value Added Tax

The payment of service charges by a tenant is regarded by HM Revenue & Customs as an additional consideration for the supply of the property by the landlord. This is irrespective of whether or not the service charge is reserved as rent in the lease.

HM Revenue & Customs will treat payment of the service charges exactly the same as rent payments for VAT purposes. VAT will be chargeable on the service charges if the landlord has elected to exercise the option to tax.

Service charge clauses normally oblige the tenant to pay any VAT that the landlord incurs as part of the services but which the landlord is unable to recover. This VAT is separate from the VAT that the tenant may be obliged to pay in relation to the service charge.

The election by the landlord to exercise the option to tax in relation to the property will mean that the landlord is unlikely to incur irrecoverable VAT.

Landlord and tenants need to be aware of their potential obligations. Tenants should also be advised that whether they can recover VAT paid to the landlord on the service charge will depend on the tenant's own VAT status.

Indexed Service Charges

Occasionally a service charge maybe of an initial specified sum and then increase in line with the retail price index or another published index each year.

There have been some problems with this approach and the intention of the clause. The drafting of indexed service charge clauses therefore needs to be very clear. If not drafted clearly, it could lead to an increase in the service charges due through an unintended cumulative effect.

Other problems arise because the published index referred to in the lease cease to exist or in the alternative, there is a change in the body in charge of the published index referred to. It cannot be assumed that in the case of bad drafting the court will come to the rescue as can be seen in the case of Arnold V Britton discussed in chapter 3.

Relevant case law

Cumshaw Ltd v Bowen [1987]

In this case the service charge payable for repairs to the roof and the main structure of the building were for an initial specified sum and then were to be increased annually in proportion to the increases in the retail price index. The clause expressly provided that if the retail price index ceased to be published or was no longer available to the public, the service charge should be computed instead by reference to the actual cost of these services.

In August 1960 the figure of the retail price index was 110.4. In the mid-1970s the government index so rebased the index figure to a new base rate figure of 100. The question was whether the landlord could invoke the changeover clause and compute the charge by referenced actual cost which would produce a higher service charge figure.

It was held that the landlord could not invoke the change-over clause. The rebasing did not mean the index had ceased. The service charge has to be calculated on the basis of the new figure.

Summary

Both the landlord and tenant should be careful when negotiating the service charge clause that if indexation is applied it meets their needs and will not potentially result in an unexpected accumulative increase or in a situation where the landlord cannot obtain the desired income. The parties also need to consider the VAT clause to ensure neither party is left in a worse position as a result of the wording of the clause.

CHAPTER NINE

MIXED USE PREMISES

Introduction

If a development/property let to commercial tenants also includes any residential units, the landlord needs to ensure they take care to comply with the relevant legislation if they wish to be able to recover the service charges due.

The position with mixed use premises

If a landlord imposes a charge in respect of a property used for both commercial and residential use, the landlord needs to comply with the more stringent rules for residential premises in respect of the residential aspects of the premises. This also applies if the residential tenant is an undertenant. The statutory controls for residential service charges are outside of the remit of this book but include section 20 consultation, dispensation, protection under the Landlord and Tenant Act 1985 and protection under the Commonhold & Leasehold Reform Act 2002.

Relevant case law

Heron Maple House Ltd v Central Estate Ltd [2002]

In this case it was established that where a landlord of a multi-let property which includes any residential unit, the leasehold interest is one to which the residential service charge consultation requirements apply.

Oakfern Properties Ltd v Ruddy [2006]

In this case it was established that residential occupiers that occupy as an undertenant cand directly challenge the service raised by the superior landlord if the superior landlord has failed to comply with the consultation requirements required for residential property.

Summary

If the landlord's development/property consist of residential units or if there are any residential occupiers either as tenants or undertenants, the landlord needs to comply with the statutory controls for residential property. Otherwise, the landlord may not be able to recover the full-service charges due.

CHAPTER TEN

VARIATIONS TO THE LEASE TERMS AND CHANGES IN IDENTITY OF THE PARTIES

Introduction

There are a number of situations where the terms of the lease may be varied or the identity of the parties to the lease may change. This chapter aims to set out various scenarios that may occur and its impact on both landlords and tenants and its effect on the recovery of service charges.

Renewal leases

The landlord or tenant may have requested that the lease be renewed under the Landlord and Tenant Act 1954. If the parties are unable to agree the service charge provisions in the new lease, the Court will determine these provisions alongside any other terms that remain in dispute.

Overriding Leases

Sometimes an overriding lease may be granted by the landlord resulting in an intermediate landlord sitting between the original landlord and the tenant. This could be an overriding lease of the entire building, or it could be of individual flats. An example of an Overriding lease arising would be overriding lease might arise for instance under section 19 of the landlord tenant bracket covenants bracket act 1995 which occurs when a landlord has pursued the previous tenant or guarantor. This is discussed at chapter 14 and is when the previous tenant or guarantor pays arrears due as a result of the current tenant's default. Once the previous tenant/guarantor has paid they are entitled to request an overriding lease under section 19 of the Landlord and Tenant (Covenants) Act 1995.

The creation of an overriding lease can create some problems in relation to obtaining payment of service charges. The overriding lease is likely to impose an obligation on the new landlord to pay to the original landlord or head landlord the same service charges as was formerly payable by the tenant. However, the tenants lease may require them to pay only 10% for example of the service costs incurred by the intermediate landlord. There is concern, that if an overriding lease is of part rather than the whole, that the tenants will only be liable to pay 10% of the sums that the intermediate landlord is paying towards the original landlord rather than 10% towards all of the service charges for the whole building. For this reason, it is important to have the relevant provisions in the lease to ensure the full-service charges paid out can be recovered from the tenants not just part. If not, it could potentially result in insolvency for the intermediate landlord.

There is also an issue in relation to landlord's covenants to provide the services and whether the tenant can require the new landlord comply with those covenants even though they may only be landlord of the individual flats or part of the building. Again, the drafting of the overriding lease needs to take this into account.

Varying the Lease

A landlord may want to change or vary or even discontinue these services which the terms of the lease expressly obliged him to provide. However, if there are no specific provisions in the lease allowing the landlord to change these services they cannot do so without agreement.

There may sometimes be good reasons for the landlord wanting to vary or discontinue a service. For example, there may have been a change in the type of services that are being provided and/or some services may have become obsolete.

If there is no provision in the lease to vary, all the landlord can do is seek the consent of the tenants as to whether they will agree to a discontinuance or substitution of the service that they are required to carry out under the lease. If agreed, there should be a formal deed of variation completed between the parties which will bind any successes if a tenant decides to assign the lease.

If all but one of the tenants agrees to the variation, then the landlord will still not be able to discontinue or substitute services as they will still be in breach of their covenant towards the tenant. If the landlord is in breach, the tenant will be able to apply for an injunction requiring the landlord to abide by their obligations in the lease and/or seek damages for the landlord's failure to carry out their obligations under the lease.

If a tenant fails to pay service charges due, a former tenant or guarantor may be liable for payment of the service charges. This is discussed in chapter 14. If a variation of the lease is agreed between the landlord and the current tenant, and as a result of the agreed variation, the amount due under the lease increases, it may be that the previous tenant/guarantor will not be liable for this increased sum.

Landlords also need to be careful about the effect of variations on the current guarantor, if there is one, as if there is a major variation which has not been agreed by the current guarantor it is likely that the guarantor will be released from its liabilities.

Assignment of the lease

If there is an assignment of the lease, the identity of the tenant will change. If the lease is registered or is required to be registered at the Land Registry the lease will not vest in the new tenant until the assignment has been registered at the Land Registry.

After completion but before registration of the assignment, the lease will remain vested in the old tenant with the new tenant having a beneficial interest. This can provide the landlord with an issue when it comes to serving any notices and/or demands for service charges. The question is who does the landlord serve for the notices/demands to be valid. In this scenario and as both the old and new tenant have an interest in the lease, it is advised that the landlord serve both the old and new tenant. Once the assignment has been registered there will be no issue and the landlord can simply proceed to serve the new tenant with all notice/demands.

As a result of the assignment the new tenant will become liable to pay the service charges under the lease and comply with those covenants that are directly between them and the landlord. However, if there is a separate management company it is necessary for the new tenant to sign a deed with them which covenants to observe the covenants and obligations. This is to ensure the management company can enforce the covenants if the tenant is in breach.

If consent for an assignment is required under the lease and the tenants does not obtain this consent, the assignment will still be valid, and the new tenant will be liable under the lease. Before treating the lease as continuing and invoicing the new tenant, the landlord may however want to consider forfeiture of the lease on the basis of the unauthorised assignment. A breach of the assignment clause is a once and for all breach so if the landlord treats the lease as continuing after it becomes aware of the assignment, it is likely to be seen that the landlord has waived its right to forfeit. The landlord would then need to accept the new tenant and treat the lease as continuing.

Relevant case law

Old Grovebury Manor Farm Ltd v Seymour Plant Sales [1979]

The lease stated that consent was required from the landlord before assigning the lease. In breach of this covenant the tenant assigned the lease without consent. The landlord became aware of the breach and served a notice pursuant to section 146 of the Law of Property Act 1925 as a precursor for forfeiting the lease. The landlord served the section 146 notice on the original defaulting tenant not the new tenant.

An assignment without consent is still a valid assignment. The lease had therefore vested in the new tenant and the new tenant was the appropriate recipient of the section 146 notice. It was held that the notice was invalid as it had been served on the incorrect party.

Is the new tenant liable for service charge arrears?

The default position is that a new tenant is not liable for arrears that accrued prior to the assignment completing. The exception to this rule is if there is a specific provision in the lease that makes the new tenant liable for unpaid service charges.

Relevant case law

Re National Jazz Centre Limited [1988]

In this case it was held that the person/company liable for sums that become due under the lease is the person/company that was the tenant when the sums became due under the lease. A person/company who became a tenant after the sums became due can only be liable if they gave the landlord a direct covenant to pay past rents and service charges. It is unusual for such a direct covenant to be given.

Investigation prior to assignment

If you are looking to take an assignment of a lease, special care should be taken in reading the service charge provisions in the lease. For example, where the provisions provide for a service charge shortfall to be paid following the issue of a certificate or account, the new tenant is likely to be liable as the arrears became due on receipt of the certificate/account even if the charges were incurred in an earlier period before the assignment completed. The important thing for tenants to review is on what date the arrears become due and if they are likely to become liable to pay the arrears.

Any person considering taking an assignment of a lease where service charges are payable should make inquiries with the current tenant and the landlord, if possible, to ascertain the following details:

1. If there has been any recent major repairs or improvements carried out for which the assignee will be liable?

2. The amount paid for service charges over the previous three years and the current estimated service charge for the current year.

3. Whether there is a reserve of sinking fund and if so, what costs this covers?

4. Whether there are any arrears of service charges?

5. Whether there are any service charge disputes?

6. Whether there is likely to be any shortfall between the amounts paid by the current tenants on account of the works and the final sums due?

The key point is that there should be a thorough investigation into the service charge position before taking an assignment of a lease.

Changes in the identity of the landlord

Having dealt with a change in the identity of the tenant, this book now moves on to the position where there is a change of the landlord.

When a landlord sells the freehold or transfers their interest in the property, the new landlord is liable to perform all of the old landlord's covenants in the lease. It is important to note though that the previous landlord is not released from its covenants in the lease, and he may have continuing liability if it has been or is in breach of those covenants. If there is any continuing liability on the old landlord to provide any services etc, it will still have the benefit of the tenants' covenants to pay the service charges of those services.

Relevant case law

Wembley National Stadium Ltd v Wembley (London) Ltd [2007]

Land at Wembley stadium had been sold to Wembley London Ltd and then leased back. Wembley (London) Ltd assigned the freehold within their group of companies and stated that the lease was held in trust for the original landlord. Wembley National Stadium Ltd then claimed that Wembley (London) Ltd was not entitled to claim the service charges due. It was held there had been an estoppel by convention which entitled Wembley (London) Ltd to claim payment of the service charges.

The new landlords right to enforce the tenant's covenants

The new landlord will be entitled to enforce the tenants' obligations under the lease. If the lease is an old tenancy, which is a lease entered into before 1st of January 1996, the landlord will have the right to pursue the tenants for service charges that accrued before it became the landlord. If it is a new tenancy, which is a lease entered into after 1st of January 1996, the default position is that new landlord can only pursue the tenants for arrears that have accrued since it acquired its interest in the property. A landlord of a new lease will, however, be able to pursue the tenant for arrears that accrued prior to it acquiring the interest in the property if the old landlord assigned to the new landlord its rights in respect of these arrears.

As with a tenant looking to take an assignment of the lease, a landlord looking to take over the freehold should also carry out thorough investigations into the service charges and the management of the building. A landlord should know if any service charges are overdue, if there is any likely large upcoming expenditure and if there are any reserve or sinking funds. A potential new landlord should also review the service charge provisions in the lease carefully, so they know their obligations in respect of service charge accounts and collection of service charges. It is surprising how many issues arise when there is a change of landlord or managing agents because the landlord or managing agent has not reviewed its obligations in the lease.

Lastly, if there is a change in landlord, the tenant should be notified. Notification is not compulsory in commercial property, however, notifying the tenants will avoid them continuing to pay service charges to the old landlord.

Summary

It is common at least in the case of longer leases, for there to be a change in the identity of the tenant or the landlord. It is also usual for leases to be renewed and as part of that renewal the terms of the existing lease to be reviewed and possibly updated. The introduction of the Code makes it more likely that landlords and tenants will seek to modernise their lease to take into consideration the Code's recommendations. Care needs to be taken in all these scenarios to ensure that the parties are aware of their obligations as a result of these changes and abide by the terms of the lease.

PART FOUR

DISPUTES AND REMEDIES

Part 1, 2 and 3 have dealt with the interpretation of service charge clauses as well as the other key points, obligations and considerations that are relevant in dealing with service charges in the commercial sector. The next logical question is how to deal with non-compliance on the part of the landlord or failure to pay on the part of the tenant. Part 4 aims to take practitioners through the various options of how to deal with service charge disputes together with the advantages and disadvantages of each option.

CHAPTER ELEVEN

ALTERNATIVE DISPUTE RESOLUTION

Introduction

The first thing to check when reviewing a service charge dispute is whether the lease provides for provision for disputes to be referred to an arbitrator or expert in the first instance. If so, the parties need to comply with this requirement. Even if it is not provided for in the lease, the parties may still want to consider ADR before going down the tribunal or Court route. This chapter sets out a brief description of a few ADR options to help decide which avenue may be appropriate in each particular case.

Referral of Disputes to an Arbitrator or Expert under the lease

There is usually provision for the lease to deal with disputes such as reference to the arbitrator or expert or it may be that the Code is adopted into the lease. As set out above one of the core principles of the Code is that all new leases (including renewal leases) should include a provision for either party to require the resolution of disputes though alternative dispute resolution.

The parties can agree which arbitrator or expert to appoint or if the parties are unable to agree, they can ask the president of the RICS or another appropriate body to appoint an arbitrator or expert.

If a commercial lease provides that a dispute over service charges should be dealt with by the landlord's surveyor this should be an independent surveyor that is unconnected to the landlord. It cannot be their managing agents, or someone connected to their managing agents as they have to be able to approach the case on a sufficiently independent basis to provide a fair outcome for both parties.

Relevant Case Law

Concorde Graphics Ltd v Andromedia Investments SA [1983].

The service charge clause provided that any difference in the sums due was to be settled by a landlord's surveyor and their decision is to be final and binding. The tenant disputed the service charge and the company that dealt with it were both the managing agents and the landlord's surveyor. It was held that the certificate of service charges they produced was not final and binding as provided for in the lease as the managing agents cannot perform the duty of deciding the difference in the service charges and what should be payable by the tenant. As managing agents, they had made the claim for service charges which the tenant was disputing. They therefore could not be seen as independent. It was held the landlord needed to appoint a different independent surveyor to determine the dispute.

Referral of Disputes to an Arbitrator or Expert if there is no provision under the lease.

If there is no provision in the lease for the matter to be referred to alternative dispute resolution, the parties can still refer the matter to a mediator or expert through agreement or referral.

ADR Procedures

There are several advantages to going down the ADR route as opposed to the Court. It is a lot more cost effective and usually leads to a quicker resolution. It is also a lot more flexible. The usual ADR procedures used are mediation, independent expert determination and arbitration.

Mediation

A mediation involves a third party that is unconnected to the dispute and therefore neutral. The aim of the arbitrator is to help the parties reach an agreement without giving their personal opinion. The third party will ask the parties to explain and clarify their positions. Usually there will be a meeting with all the parties and the mediator present at the beginning of the mediation, but mediation can take place with both parties remaining in separate rooms throughout if required. A good mediator will be able to suggest ways forward and possible satisfactory solutions. Mediation is unlikely to work if the parties are not willing to enter into a dialogue, negotiate and move from their starting position.

Independent expert determination

This is a process by which an independent third-party acts as an expert in the field rather than a judge or arbitrator. The parties can agree the expert to be appointed or refer it to an appointing body such as the CIArb. The expert will hear evidence from both parties and then makes a decision which is binding. The decision is confidential.

Arbitration

This is a more formal procedure which is similar to Court proceedings. The parties can agree who to appoint or apply for one to be appointed. The arbitrator will set directions for submissions and evidence. The arbitrator will then make an award which binds the parties. The parties can apply to Court to enforce the award if the parties fail to comply with the contents. Although more formal, arbitration is a lot more flexible than court proceedings and at less cost.

The Code recommends mediation or an independent expert determination for service charge disputes.

Summary

Settling a matter through ADR is a much more appealing option for both landlords and tenants. In addition, if one party does offer ADR, it is expected that the other party will accept this offer. Failure to do so could lead to cost consequences if the matter proceeds to trial.

CHAPTER TWELVE

APPLICATION FOR A DECLARATION

Introduction

If a landlord is unsure of whether a service charge is payable under the terms of the lease, it is open for the landlord to apply to the Court for a declaration on the interpretation of the service charge clause or the correctness/accuracy of a service charge calculation or certificate. This process has been encouraged in a number of cases.

When would a declaration be applicable?

Prior to applying to the Court, the landlord will want to seek the tenant's agreement to the service charges or the certificate/calculation. If they cannot be agreed and the landlord is uncertain that the service charges are payable i.e., if the sweeper clause is unclear, the landlord may want to seek a declaration before incurring the costs of works which they may not be able to recover. If a landlord simply goes ahead with works that they are unsure are covered by the service charge clause, they risk a dispute from the tenants regarding liability and ultimately the risk that the service charges will not be payable. This could leave a landlord or a managing company in a very difficult position financially.

Costs

The costs of the Court application can be included in the service charge if the lease sets out that the costs of management or for management to discharge their liabilities are recoverable from the tenant.

Relevant Case

Reston Ltd v Hudson [1990]

In this case the landlord proposed to replace all of the window frames in a block of flats. However, not all of them were in disrepair at the time. It made sense for the landlord to carry out repairs on the window frames of the whole block. The other windows were likely to fall into disrepair shortly and to carry out the repair in bulk would be cheaper than in 2 or more occasions. The landlord was concerned that they might not be able to recover the sums incurred if not all the windows were in disrepair so they applied to the tribunal to determine if the tenants would be liable for the full sums. It was held that the landlord could replace all of the window frames and recover the full costs incurred from the tenants.

Summary

Landlords should carefully consider issuing a claim for a declaration that particular service charges are payable if the wording in the lease is unclear to prevent possible financial loss if they are not recoverable.

CHAPTER THIRTEEN

TENANT'S REMEDIES FOR NON-PERFORMANCE OF THE LANDLORD'S OBLIGATIONS

Introduction

The landlords' obligations under the legislation to enable them to claim service charges has been discussed at length. However, what happens if the landlord just fails to carry out the repairs they are obliged to do under the lease and what can the tenant do in those circumstances? This chapter sets out the possible options available to tenants.

Application for an injunction to force the landlord to carry out works

To proceed down this avenue there needs to be an urgency to the works, or the disrepair needs to be very severe. It is only advisable in exceptional circumstances as the tenant is asking the Court to order an interim injunction in the first instance. A Court will need to determine if this is applicable without the matter being fully argued at Trial. The tenant would need to have significant evidence including a surveyor's report or expert evidence showing the works are needed immediately. If an interim injunction is granted the matter will then be listed for directions and a hearing to decide a final injunction should be ordered.

Issue a claim for damages

The tenant can issue a claim for damages resulting from the landlord's failure to repair. Prior to issuing proceedings, the tenant will need to have contacted the landlord and given them a reasonable time to comply with their covenants. The losses claimed must be reasonably foreseeable and compensation will only be payable from the date on which the Landlord had knowledge of disrepair. The amount awarded will depend on the losses that have actually been suffered.

Payment of service charges due whilst a dispute is ongoing

Tenants will not want to pay service charges that they dispute are payable. However, they may also want to prevent action being initiated against them for payment such as forfeiture for non-payment of the service charges. The RICS Service Charge Code advises tenants to pay the sums properly demanded and only withhold payment of the sums disputed.

The alternative is for the tenant to pay all the service charges due including those in dispute but to pay them on a without prejudice to the position to the disputed sums and also state that they are reserving their right to dispute the service charges in due course.

Summary

A tenant should only consider the first option in severe circumstances. In both instances the tenant should have approached the landlord to do the works and given them reasonable time to do so. What is reasonable obviously depends on the urgency of the works. Tenants should also be careful when withholding service charge payments.

CHAPTER FOURTEEN

LANDLORD'S REMEDIES FOR NON-PAYMENT OF SERVICE CHARGES

Introduction

If the tenant has failed to pay the service charges, the landlord needs to be able to enforce the right to recover the sums due. The landlord is no longer able to distain for service charges which are reserved as rent under the lease as this was abolished as from 6 April 2014. The landlord does however have recourse through the Courts for recovery of the sums due either through issuing forfeiture proceedings or a debt claim.

Forfeiture of the lease

If a landlord wishes to seek possession on grounds of non-payment of service charges, they must first serve a notice under section 146 of the Law of Property Act 1925. This notice must set out the tenant's breach of their lease and require the tenant to pay the service charges due within a reasonable time. A reasonable time is likely to be between 14 and 28 days.

A section 146 notice is not required if the service charges are specified as being reserved as rent within the lease as forfeiture for nonpayment of rent is excluded from section 146 of the Law of Property Act 1925.

If a section 146 notice id not required or the tenant fails to pay within the reasonable time specified in the section 146 notice, the landlord can then issue forfeiture proceedings at the Court. Failure to pay service charges is a one and for all breach so landlords need to be careful to not waive their right to forfeit once the right has arisen. The landlord should therefore not treat the lease as continuing. For example, no further demands for payment for service charges or rent should be sent to the tenant once the right to forfeit has arisen.

Once proceedings have been issued by the Court the Court will list the matter for a hearing. At the hearing a possession order can be requested. If a possession order is granted, there is still a possibility that a tenant may apply for relief from forfeiture by paying the service charges due together with costs.

Landlords of commercial property do have the option of forfeiture by peaceable re-entry but there is a risk that it could be held as unlawful if it is later found that the service charges are not due from the tenant. This could result in the tenant taking action against the landlord for trespass and a substantial claim for damages. If there is any dispute over whether the service charge is payable forfeiture by peaceable re-entry will not be the appropriate course of action.

Landlords cannot forfeit on the basis of service charges in mixed use premises until either the tenant's liability for service charges has been determined by the Court, tribunal or arbitrator or if the tenant has admitted liability under section 81(1) of the Housing Act 1996.

Issue court proceedings for recovery of the service charge arrears

Service charges will only become due once all the procedures and obligations under the lease have been complied with regarding payment of the arrears.

Relevant cases

Canary Riverside PTE Ltd v Schilling [2005]

The lease provided that the landlord had to give the tenant written notice of any revised estimate of the annual service costs if it exceeded the previously notified estimate. The landlord incurred significant costs above their initial estimate and claimed the additional costs without providing the revised estimate. It was held that the landlord could not recover the additional sums incurred as they had failed to comply with the procedure in the lease.

Warrior Quay Management Company Limited v Joachim [2008]

The lease provided that the landlord was to provide audited accounts in order for the tenants to be liable for any balancing charges. The landlord failed to provide the audited accounts and issued proceedings. It was held that the landlord could not issue for recovery of the charges until such time as they had complied with the requirements under the lease and served the audited accounts.

Once the landlord has complied with any preconditions in the lease, it is advisable that the landlord then serves a letter before action on the tenant providing them with 30 days to reply to the Claim. This is more essential if the landlord is a company and is acting against an individual. If no response is received on the expiry of the letter before action or matters do not progress after the initial response the landlord can then issue proceedings. There will be Court issue fee payable, the sum of which will depend on the value of the claim. Once the claim has been issued and served the tenant will have 14 days to file and acknowledgment of service as with any debt claim. If the tenant fails to do so or fails to file a defence 14 days after the acknowledgment of service, the landlord can request judgment. If the tenant does file a defence, the Court will list the case for directions and a trial. If a defence is filed, the proceedings will become very lengthy and costly.

Once a judgement is obtained it is a matter of considering how the landlord can enforce. This is where the tenant's financial situation is key. If the tenant does not have the funds to pay the judgment it may be that the landlord will be throwing good money after bad in trying to recoup the same. However, in most cases, I would expect the tenant to at least have a leasehold interest which a landlord could consider obtaining a charge over for the sums due. The other routes a landlord may consider are serving a statutory demand on the tenant (if the sums due are over £5,000), a warrant of execution or an attachment of earnings. The best method of enforcement will depend on the circumstances of the case, and it may be worthwhile instructing an enquiry agent to carry out an asset sweep on the tenant in the first instance to assist in deciding the best method of enforcement.

Relevant cases

Commerz Real Investment gesellschaft MBH v TFS Stores Ltd [2021]

It was held that a landlord was entitled to summary judgement against its tenant for non-payment of rent and service charges during the COVID-19 pandemic.

Can the tenant set off damages from the service charges demanded for breach of the landlord's covenants?

If the landlord is in breach of covenant, the tenant can set off their damages claim against the sums due to the landlord under the lease even if the damages claim is unliquidated at the time the sums became fully payable. An example is where the tenant claims service charges have been increased due to the landlord's failure to carry out necessary works as appropriate. However, the Court has the discretion whether or not to allow the tenant to do so and may not allow it if the tenant's conduct is considered unfair. The tenant can also not offset damages against the service charges due if the lease expressly prohibits any set off from the service charge and in modern leases, offset is usually excluded.

Action against Previous Tenants

The lease is a contract between the landlord and tenant and the original tenant and/or guarantor is likely to remain bound to pay service charge in case of the tenant's default through the entire term of the lease.

If it is an old lease, which is a lease before 1 January 1996, all the old tenants and guarantors will be liable. If it is a new lease, which is a lease after 1 January 1996, the previous tenant/guarantor needs to have signed an authorised guarantee agreement.

If a previous tenant/guarantor is liable the landlord needs to serve a notice under section 17 of the Landlord and Tenant (Covenants) Act 1995 within 6 months of the service charges becoming due.

If the landlord does not serve a section 17 notice within 6 months of the service charges becoming due, the landlord will have no course of action for these arrears.

If a section 17 notice is served and the tenant fails to pay the sums demanded the landlord can then proceed to issue Court proceedings with a view to obtaining judgment. The procedure to obtain judgment will be as set out above on issuing proceedings for the sums due against the tenant.

Summary

If a tenant has failed to pay service charges, the landlord has two main options after exploring alternative dispute resolution which is either forfeiture or issuing proceedings for recovery of the sums due. The best option will depend on the circumstances.

CHAPTER FIFTEEN

LEGAL COSTS

Introduction

If the landlord issues proceedings for arrears of service charge through the Court and obtains a judgment, the usual position is that the landlord will be awarded costs from the tenant. There can be come variation from this position though and the wording of the lease can also be relevant.

Recovery of costs

The recovery of legal costs through the court is not clear cut is ultimately usually down to the discretion of the court and what they consider to be just and equitable in the circumstances. Costs are usually awarded on a standard basis and less than the actual costs incurred. However, this is not the case in small claims matters where each party will bear their own costs. Costs can also be awarded on an indemnity basis if the judge considers it appropriate. This is usually if the judge considers one party has acted unreasonably. If a lease provides that the costs should be given on an indemnity basis the judge will give this weight, but it is not conclusive.

To assist in understanding the recovery of legal costs some cases are detailed below.

Relevant cases

Sella House Ltd v Mears [1989]

The lease allowed the recovery through the service charges of the costs of collecting the rent and employing professional persons for the administration of the building. The landlord argued that this covered his legal costs. It was held that the wording of the service charge clause should be clear and unambiguous to allow recovery of legal costs. This clause did not specificallly provide for legal costs and they were not recoverable.

Iperion Investments Corporation v Broadwalk House Residents Ltd [1995]

The lease provided for payment of:

> "All costs ... properly incurred by the Landlord in carrying out its obligations ... under the covenants and conditions contained in the Head Lease ... and in the proper and reasonable management of [the property]."

The Court of Appeal held that under this clause the landlord could recover the legal costs incurred as a result of managing the property.

Plantation Wharf Management Company Ltd v Jackson and another [2011]

The lease permitted the recovery of professional advisers' fees relating to the enforcement of covenants. It was held that the management company could recover its legal costs through the service charge, despite the fact the clause did not explicitly include the words "legal costs". This case illustrates that the absence of an express reference may not be fatal to the recovery of legal costs. The case also commented that when asked by a tenant to make a section 20 direction, the risk of a management company becoming insolvent is a relevant consideration.

Shearbarn Holiday Park Ltd v Wornell and others [2021]

A court order stated there was to be no order as to costs. The service charge clause in the lease stated that litigation costs could be recovered. It was held that the provision for recovery in the lease was overridden by the provision in the consent order stating there was to be no order as to costs. Whether this is the case in other matters, however, is going to be highly dependent on the facts of a particular case and the background to the consent order.

Criterion Buildings Ltd v McKinsey & Company Inc (United Kingdom) and another [2021]

The landlord was successful in obtaining judgment against the tenant for unpaid service charges. The Court then had to consider how to deal with costs. There was provision in the lease and supplemental lease that the tenant was to pay landlord's expenses "properly incurred" and "all costs, charges and expenses which the landlord may from time to time incur...". It was held that the covenants in the lease and supplemental lease justified an order for the landlord's costs of the proceedings to be recovered as service charges and to be assessed on the indemnity basis.

Summary

There is no clear position on costs and whether costs are likely to be recovered will depend on an assessment of the wording of the relevant clauses in the lease and the parties' conduct.

CHAPTER SIXTEEN

SUMMARY

This book has aimed to provide you with guidance on how to approach commercial service charge clauses and deal with commercial service charge disputes. Hopefully, the contents will assist as a starting point if you are approached with any commercial service charge queries.

There is no legislation in respect of commercial service charges so there is a heavy reliance on the construction of the service charge clause and case law. However, the Code should always be considered and adhered to when ever possible and provides guidance to all practitioners in this area.

There are no current proposed changes in how commercial service charges are dealt with. At some point a new or revised service charge code may be introduced with further recommendations, but it is not known when or if this will happen.

MORE BOOKS BY LAW BRIEF PUBLISHING

A selection of our other titles available now:-

'A Practical Guide to Estate Administration and Crypto Assets' by Richard Marshall
'A Practical Guide to Managing GDPR Data Subject Access Requests – Second Edition' by Patrick O'Kane
'A Practical Guide to Parental Alienation in Private and Public Law Children Cases' by Sam King QC & Frankie Shama
'Contested Heritage – Removing Art from Land and Historic Buildings' by Richard Harwood QC, Catherine Dobson, David Sawtell
'The Limits of Separate Legal Personality: When Those Running a Company Can Be Held Personally Liable for Losses Caused to Third Parties Outside of the Company' by Dr Mike Wilkinson
'A Practical Guide to Transgender Law' by Robin Moira White & Nicola Newbegin
'Artificial Intelligence – The Practical Legal Issues (2nd Edition)' by John Buyers
'A Practical Guide to Residential Freehold Conveyancing' by Lorraine Richardson
'A Practical Guide to Pensions on Divorce for Lawyers' by Bryan Scant
'A Practical Guide to Challenging Sham Marriage Allegations in Immigration Law' by Priya Solanki
'A Practical Guide to Legal Rights in Scotland' by Sarah-Jane Macdonald
'A Practical Guide to New Build Conveyancing' by Paul Sams & Rebecca East
'A Practical Guide to Defending Barristers in Disciplinary Cases' by Marc Beaumont
'A Practical Guide to Inherited Wealth on Divorce' by Hayley Trim
'A Practical Guide to Practice Direction 12J and Domestic Abuse in Private Law Children Proceedings' by Rebecca Cross & Malvika Jaganmohan
'A Practical Guide to Confiscation and Restraint' by Narita Bahra QC, John Carl Townsend, David Winch
'A Practical Guide to the Law of Forests in Scotland' by Philip Buchan
'A Practical Guide to Health and Medical Cases in Immigration Law' by Rebecca Chapman & Miranda Butler

'A Practical Guide to Bad Character Evidence for Criminal Practitioners by Aparna Rao
'A Practical Guide to Extradition Law post-Brexit' by Myles Grandison et al
'A Practical Guide to Hoarding and Mental Health for Housing Lawyers' by Rachel Coyle
'A Practical Guide to Psychiatric Claims in Personal Injury – 2nd Edition' by Liam Ryan
'Stephens on Contractual Indemnities' by Richard Stephens
'A Practical Guide to the EU Succession Regulation' by Richard Frimston
'A Practical Guide to Solicitor and Client Costs – 2nd Edition' by Robin Dunne
'Constructive Dismissal – Practice Pointers and Principles' by Benjimin Burgher
'A Practical Guide to Religion and Belief Discrimination Claims in the Workplace' by Kashif Ali
'A Practical Guide to the Law of Medical Treatment Decisions' by Ben Troke
'Fundamental Dishonesty and QOCS in Personal Injury Proceedings: Law and Practice' by Jake Rowley
'A Practical Guide to the Law in Relation to School Exclusions' by Charlotte Hadfield & Alice de Coverley
'A Practical Guide to Divorce for the Silver Separators' by Karin Walker
'The Right to be Forgotten – The Law and Practical Issues' by Melissa Stock
'A Practical Guide to Planning Law and Rights of Way in National Parks, the Broads and AONBs' by James Maurici QC, James Neill et al
'A Practical Guide to Election Law' by Tom Tabori
'A Practical Guide to the Law in Relation to Surrogacy' by Andrew Powell
'A Practical Guide to Claims Arising from Fatal Accidents – 2nd Edition' by James Patience
'A Practical Guide to the Ownership of Employee Inventions – From Entitlement to Compensation' by James Tumbridge & Ashley Roughton
'A Practical Guide to Asbestos Claims' by Jonathan Owen & Gareth McAloon
'A Practical Guide to Stamp Duty Land Tax in England and Northern Ireland' by Suzanne O'Hara
'A Practical Guide to the Law of Farming Partnerships' by Philip Whitcomb
'Covid-19, Homeworking and the Law – The Essential Guide to Employment and GDPR Issues' by Forbes Solicitors
'Covid-19 and Criminal Law – The Essential Guide' by Ramya Nagesh

'Covid-19 and Family Law in England and Wales – The Essential Guide' by Safda Mahmood
'A Practical Guide to the Law of Unlawful Eviction and Harassment – 2nd Edition' by Stephanie Lovegrove
'Covid-19, Brexit and the Law of Commercial Leases – The Essential Guide' by Mark Shelton
'A Practical Guide to Costs in Personal Injury Claims – 2nd Edition' by Matthew Hoe
'A Practical Guide to the General Data Protection Regulation (GDPR) – 2nd Edition' by Keith Markham
'Ellis on Credit Hire – Sixth Edition' by Aidan Ellis & Tim Kevan
'A Practical Guide to Working with Litigants in Person and McKenzie Friends in Family Cases' by Stuart Barlow
'Protecting Unregistered Brands: A Practical Guide to the Law of Passing Off' by Lorna Brazell
'A Practical Guide to Secondary Liability and Joint Enterprise Post-Jogee' by Joanne Cecil & James Mehigan
'A Practical Guide to the Pre-Action RTA Claims Protocol for Personal Injury Lawyers' by Antonia Ford
'A Practical Guide to Neighbour Disputes and the Law' by Alexander Walsh
'A Practical Guide to Forfeiture of Leases' by Mark Shelton
'A Practical Guide to Coercive Control for Legal Practitioners and Victims' by Rachel Horman
'A Practical Guide to Rights Over Airspace and Subsoil' by Daniel Gatty
'Tackling Disclosure in the Criminal Courts – A Practitioner's Guide' by Narita Bahra QC & Don Ramble
'A Practical Guide to the Law of Driverless Cars – Second Edition' by Alex Glassbrook, Emma Northey & Scarlett Milligan
'A Practical Guide to TOLATA Claims' by Greg Williams
'A Practical Guide to Elderly Law – 2nd Edition' by Justin Patten
'A Practical Guide to Responding to Housing Disrepair and Unfitness Claims' by Iain Wightwick
'A Practical Guide to the Construction and Rectification of Wills and Trust Instruments' by Edward Hewitt
'A Practical Guide to the Law of Bullying and Harassment in the Workplace' by Philip Hyland

'How to Be a Freelance Solicitor: A Practical Guide to the SRA-Regulated Freelance Solicitor Model' by Paul Bennett
'A Practical Guide to Prison Injury Claims' by Malcolm Johnson
'A Practical Guide to the Small Claims Track - 2nd Edition' by Dominic Bright
'A Practical Guide to Advising Clients at the Police Station' by Colin Stephen McKeown-Beaumont
'A Practical Guide to Antisocial Behaviour Injunctions' by Iain Wightwick
'Practical Mediation: A Guide for Mediators, Advocates, Advisers, Lawyers, and Students in Civil, Commercial, Business, Property, Workplace, and Employment Cases' by Jonathan Dingle with John Sephton
'The Mini-Pupillage Workbook' by David Boyle
'A Practical Guide to Crofting Law' by Brian Inkster
'A Practical Guide to Spousal Maintenance' by Liz Cowell
'A Practical Guide to the Law of Domain Names and Cybersquatting' by Andrew Clemson
'A Practical Guide to the Law of Gender Pay Gap Reporting' by Harini Iyengar
'NHS Whistleblowing and the Law' by Joseph England
'Employment Law and the Gig Economy' by Nigel Mackay & Annie Powell
'A Practical Guide to Noise Induced Hearing Loss (NIHL) Claims' by Andrew Mckie, Ian Skeate, Gareth McAloon
'An Introduction to Beauty Negligence Claims – A Practical Guide for the Personal Injury Practitioner' by Greg Almond
'Intercompany Agreements for Transfer Pricing Compliance' by Paul Sutton
'Zen and the Art of Mediation' by Martin Plowman
'A Practical Guide to the SRA Principles, Individual and Law Firm Codes of Conduct 2019 – What Every Law Firm Needs to Know' by Paul Bennett
'A Practical Guide to Adoption for Family Lawyers' by Graham Pegg
'A Practical Guide to Industrial Disease Claims' by Andrew Mckie & Ian Skeate
'A Practical Guide to Redundancy' by Philip Hyland
'A Practical Guide to Vicarious Liability' by Mariel Irvine
'A Practical Guide to Applications for Landlord's Consent and Variation of Leases' by Mark Shelton
'A Practical Guide to Relief from Sanctions Post-Mitchell and Denton' by Peter Causton

'A Practical Guide to Equity Release for Advisors' by Paul Sams
'A Practical Guide to Financial Services Claims' by Chris Hegarty
'The Law of Houses in Multiple Occupation: A Practical Guide to HMO Proceedings' by Julian Hunt
'Occupiers, Highways and Defective Premises Claims: A Practical Guide Post-Jackson – 2nd Edition' by Andrew Mckie
'A Practical Guide to Financial Ombudsman Service Claims' by Adam Temple & Robert Scrivenor
'A Practical Guide to Advising Schools on Employment Law' by Jonathan Holden
'A Practical Guide to Running Housing Disrepair and Cavity Wall Claims: 2nd Edition' by Andrew Mckie & Ian Skeate
'A Practical Guide to Holiday Sickness Claims – 2nd Edition' by Andrew Mckie & Ian Skeate
'Arguments and Tactics for Personal Injury and Clinical Negligence Claims' by Dorian Williams
'A Practical Guide to Drone Law' by Rufus Ballaster, Andrew Firman, Eleanor Clot
'A Practical Guide to Compliance for Personal Injury Firms Working With Claims Management Companies' by Paul Bennett
'RTA Allegations of Fraud in a Post-Jackson Era: The Handbook – 2nd Edition' by Andrew Mckie
'RTA Personal Injury Claims: A Practical Guide Post-Jackson' by Andrew Mckie
'On Experts: CPR35 for Lawyers and Experts' by David Boyle
'An Introduction to Personal Injury Law' by David Boyle

These books and more are available to order online direct from the publisher at www.lawbriefpublishing.com, where you can also read free sample chapters. For any queries, contact us on 0844 587 2383 or mail@lawbriefpublishing.com.

Our books are also usually in stock at www.amazon.co.uk with free next day delivery for Prime members, and at good legal bookshops such as Wildy & Sons.

We are regularly launching new books in our series of practical day-to-day practitioners' guides. Visit our website and join our free newsletter to be kept informed and to receive special offers, free chapters, etc.

You can also follow us on Twitter at www.twitter.com/lawbriefpub.

Printed in Dunstable, United Kingdom

64773597R00060